PART ONE

RUSSIA UNDER THE TSAR

Russian women towing a barge on the river Volga, around the turn of the century

In 1899, not long before this photograph was taken, a twenty-nine year old Russian wrote

> 'The Russian working class is burdened by a double yoke; it is . . . robbed by the capitalists and landlords, and to prevent it from fighting them, the police bind it hand and foot, gag it, and persecute every attempt to defend the rights of the people.'

The writer, Vladimir Ilyich Lenin, was not at that moment watching these women hauling a barge on the river Volga. He was thousands of miles away in Siberia, the eastern part of Russia, where he had been sent as a punishment for helping workers to organise a strike. But it was exactly the kind of scene Lenin might have had in mind when he wrote these words about the workers of Russia. And the thought of workers having to put up with conditions like these made Lenin determined to overthrow the Russian government and to provide the Russian people with a new way of life.

Part One of this book shows why conditions for many Russian people were so bad at the start of this century, and why the Russian government did little to improve them. Part Two shows how Lenin, twenty years after he wrote the words above, succeeded in overthrowing the government. Part Three describes how he became the ruler of Russia and invites you to decide whether he provided a better system than the one he overthrew.

1

THE RUSSIAN EMPIRE IN 1900

Russia is very, very big. You could fit all of the British Isles into Russia ninety times over. It takes over a week in an express train, travelling day and night, to get from Moscow in the west to Vladivostok in the east. Russia is so big that the sun rises in the far east of the country at the same time as it sets in the west.

The land and the climate

Much of Russia is covered by thick pine forest called 'taiga'. This scene in the taiga was photographed in 1880

Although Russia is vast, much of the land is quite useless. Study the map opposite and you will quickly see why. Look first at the southern border. The high mountains there are a good defence against foreign invaders, but they also keep out warm air trying to spread from the south. This leaves Russia open to cold air sweeping down from the Arctic Ocean. For this reason Russia is mostly useless for farming. In the Arctic Circle the land is 'tundra' where nothing grows except moss and small shrubs. For more than

1000 kilometres south of the tundra stretches the 'taiga', cold land covered in forests of pine trees. It is only in the warmer regions of the south-west that the soil can be used for farming. In 1900 only 5 per cent of all Russian land was used for farming: the rest lay waste.

The cold climate affected Russia's industry and commerce as well as her farming. Look on the map at Russia's long coastline. Much of it is inside the Arctic circle and is therefore frozen over with thick ice for much of the year. So too are the great rivers of Siberia – the Ob, the Yenisey and the Lena. Today, massive ice-breaking ships smash channels through the ice for other ships to use, but in 1900 the ice-breakers were not so powerful. The coast and the rivers stayed locked in ice throughout the long winter, so sea and river trade were impossible until spring arrived. A new railway, the Trans-Siberian, was being built to allow trade between east and west all year round, but in 1900 it was still only half-built.

An empire of many peoples

In 1900 Russia was a great empire ruled by a **Tsar**, or Emperor – Nicholas II. About 125 million people lived in Tsar Nicholas's empire. As you can see from the table below less than half were Russians.

Population of the Russian Empire, according to a census in 1897

Russians	55,650,000
Ukrainians	22,400,000
Poles	7,900,000
Byelorussians	5,900,000
Jews	5,000,000
Kirghiz	4,000,000
Tartars	3,700,000
Finns	2,500,000
Germans	1,800,000
Lithuanians	1,650,000
Letts	1,400,000
Georgians	1,350,000
Armenians	1,150,000
Romanians	1,110,000
Caucasians	1,000,000
Estonians	1,000,000
Iranians	1,000,000
Other Asiatic peoples	5,750,000
Mongols	500,000
Others	200,000

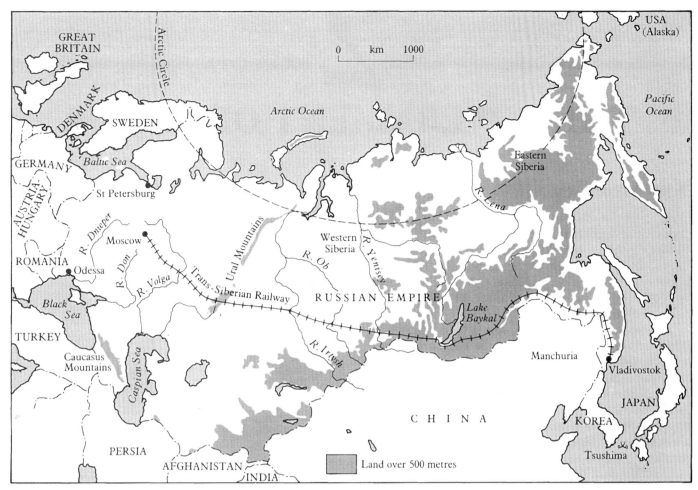

The Russian Empire in 1900

The majority were peoples such as the Poles and the Ukrainians who had been conquered by the ancestors of Tsar Nicholas II. These peoples each had their own language, their own customs and their own way of life. So for six out of ten of the Tsar's subjects Russian was a foreign language and Russian people were foreigners.

The many peoples of the Russian Empire were not spread evenly throughout the country. Most lived on the 5 per cent of land that was good for farming. The cold lands of Siberia, east of the Ural mountains, were therefore thinly populated, while the fertile land of the south-west and the streets of the cities were often overcrowded.

Work section

A. Make a table like the one below. Then use the information in the map above to fill each column.

Countries neighbouring Russia	Seas and oceans around Russia	Major rivers in Russia	Mountain ranges in Russia
(Total = 12)	(Total = 5)	(Total = 7)	(Total = 2)

B. Make a list of the advantages that you think a country like Russia has in being big. What do you think are the disadvantages in a country being as big as Russia? Consider such factors as transport, defence, natural resources etc.

C. Study the table opposite of the population of the Russian Empire, then answer these questions:
  1. a) How many Russians lived in the Empire?
     b) How many non-Russian people lived in the Empire?
  2. What difficulties do you think Tsar Nicholas might have faced in governing so many different nationalities?
  3. What problems do you think faced the non-Russian people of the Empire in being governed by a Russian Tsar?

THE GOVERNMENT OF RUSSIA

The autocracy

Tsar Nicholas II, the Emperor of Russia, was an **autocrat** – a monarch who does not have to share power. Nicholas could make new laws, increase taxes, do exactly what he liked, without consulting anyone. There was no parliament to limit his power, and he could sack any minister or adviser who disagreed with him.

In practice Nicholas could not govern 125 million Russians all by himself. To run the affairs of his vast empire the Tsar employed many thousands of civil servants. They were organised like an army into fourteen ranks. At the top of the 'Table of Ranks' were ministers in charge of government departments. At the bottom were minor officials, such as post office clerks and customs inspectors. The Tsar's civil service collected taxes from the Russian people and made sure that his decisions were carried out. And because they were underpaid for their work, many civil servants made ends meet by taking bribes.

The Tsar did not allow people to question his authority or challenge his power. To make sure that nobody opposed him, Nicholas had a secret police force, the **Okhrana**, or 'Protective Section'. The Okhrana censored all books and newspapers. Its agents spied on political groups and arrested people who criticised the government. Political prisoners were tried by special courts without juries, and usually ended up in exile. This means that they, like Lenin (whom you met on page 1) were punished by being sent to live in the cold lands of Siberia.

Sometimes, especially when there was famine, the Okhrana could not cope with all the opponents of the Tsar, and riots broke out. Workers in factories went on strike and peasants in the country attacked their landlords or the tax collectors. When this happened it was the **Cossacks** who came to the Tsar's rescue. Cossacks were fierce mounted soldiers armed with sabres who specialised in breaking up mobs by butchering anyone not able to run away fast enough.

In a different way the church in Russia also helped to maintain the authority of the Tsar. The priests of the **Russian Orthodox Church** taught people to respect the autocracy and to be loyal to the Tsar. The head of the church was a government minister. Bishops took their orders from him and priests took their orders from the bishops. In this way the government had control over the minds and souls of many Russian churchgoers.

Nicholas and Alexandra

So what kind of man was Nicholas II, the 'Tsar and Autocrat of all the Russias', as his official title described him? These extracts should give you some idea of his character:

A. Nicholas had this to say in October 1894, the day after the death of his father, Alexander III:

'What is going to happen to me, to all Russia? I am not ready to be the Tsar. I never wanted to become one. I know nothing of the business of ruling. I have no idea of even how to talk to ministers.'

B. In January 1895 Nicholas said:

'I shall preserve the principle of autocracy just as firmly . . . as my late unforgettable father preserved it.'

C. Count Witte, Russia's first Prime Minister, was sacked by Nicholas in 1906. This is how it happened:

'We talked for two solid hours. He shook my hand. He wished me all the luck in the world. I went home beside myself with happiness and found a written order for my dismissal lying on my desk.'

Tsar Nicholas II (left) and his son Alexis, 1913. Alexis is being carried by a Cossack officer

A cavalry charge by the dreaded Cossacks in Habarovsk, Siberia

D. Sir Arthur Nicholson was the British Ambassador to Russia in 1906. Here he describes Nicholas II:

'The gentle but uneducated Emperor . . . is weak on every point except his own autocracy.'

E. Alexander Kerensky, Russian politician and Prime Minister in 1917, wrote about Nicholas in his memoirs in 1966:

'The daily work of a ruler he found terribly boring. He could not stand listening long or seriously to ministers' reports, or reading them. He liked such ministers as could tell an amusing story and did not weary his attention with too much business.'

Nicholas's German wife, Alexandra, was confident and strong willed. From the start of his reign she encouraged Nicholas to rule as an autocrat and to ignore new ideas about sharing power with the people.

Nicholas and Alexandra were very happily married, and had five children during the first ten years of their marriage. The first four were girls and the fifth was a boy, Alexis, the heir to the throne. But the happiness of Nicholas and Alexandra was ruined when they found out shortly after he was born that Alexis had a blood disease, haemophilia, which prevented his blood from clotting. There was no cure for haemophilia, and even a small cut could cause Alexis to bleed to death. A slight bump could lead to massive internal swellings and agonising pain.

Both Nicholas and Alexandra were deeply religious. Alexandra had a chapel specially built in the grounds of the royal palace and every day she prayed there for hours, begging for the recovery of her son. In the meantime she ordered her daughters never to talk about Alexis's illness and made everyone else who knew about it swear an oath of secrecy.

Work section

A. Test your understanding of this chapter by explaining the meanings of the following words: autocrat, Tsar, Okhrana, Cossacks, haemophilia.

B. Study the photograph of Tsar Nicholas II and his son Alexis on the opposite page. Using the information you have read in this chapter, answer these questions:
1. What disease was Alexis suffering from, and what were its effects?
2. Why do you think Alexis was being carried by a Cossack officer?
3. Why do you think Alexandra made her son's illness into a state secret?

C. Read extracts A to E on the character and ideas of Nicholas II.
1. Write a paragraph in your own words, describing the character and ideas of Nicholas II.
2. Which of these extracts do you trust most as historical evidence? Which do you trust least? Explain both your answers.

D. Before going any further, make revision notes on what you have read so far in this book. If you are unsure about how to organise your notes, use points A and B of the revision guide on page 14 to help you.

3

RUSSIAN SOCIETY

The peasants

In 1900 four out of every five citizens of the Russian Empire were peasants – country people who made their living by farming. Until 1861 the peasants had been **serfs**, slaves of their landlords with no rights, no freedom and no land of their own.

In 1861, Tsar Alexander II, Nicholas II's grandfather, freed the peasants from serfdom and allowed them to own the land on which they grew their food. But there were strings attached to this deal. First, the land on which the peasants grew their food was not given to them as individuals: it was given to the village commune, or **mir**, in which they lived. Second, the peasants had to pay for the land given to the commune in yearly instalments, called redemption payments, over the next forty-nine years. Only when a peasant had paid all forty-nine instalments would the land become his or her personal property.

Being freed from serfdom on these conditions did not improve the lives of the peasants. Each year the mirs divided up the land in the communes and gave it out to each family according to its needs that year: the bigger the family, the bigger the plot of land it was given. But as each year went by, and as the population grew, the plots of land grew smaller and smaller. Between 1861 and 1900 the average size of plots halved. This meant that peasants found it harder each year to support their families. And at the same time they had to keep up with the yearly redemption payments for the land they did not yet own.

For all these reasons life for Russian peasants was hard. Nearly half of all new-born children died before the age of five, while the average life expectancy of those who did reach the age of five was only fifty years. Diseases and malnutrition were very common. The best that peasants could hope for in life was a good harvest. Then they would have enough to eat – mostly bread and root vegetables – and a little extra to sell at market so that they could pay their taxes and redemption payments for the year.

The town workers

Many peasants tried to improve their lives by going to work in the nearest town or city. There they would work in factories or mines until harvest time, when they returned to their communes.

A boarding house in Moscow, 1911

The largest city in Russia in 1900 was the capital, St Petersburg (see map on page 3). Nearly a million people had come there in search of work and the number was still growing. This extract from a book written in 1905 by Father Georgei Gapon, a priest in St Petersburg, gives a clear idea of what life was like for cotton workers in the city.

'They receive miserable wages and generally live in an overcrowded state, very commonly in special lodging houses. A woman takes several rooms in her own name, subletting each one; and it is common to see ten or more persons living in one room and four sleeping in one bed.

The normal working day is eleven and a half hours of work, exclusive of meal times. But . . . manufacturers have received permission to work overtime, so that the average day is longer than that nominally allowed by law – fourteen or fifteen hours. I often watched the crowds of poorly clad and emaciated [*very thin*] figures of men and girls returning from the mills . . . Why do they agree to work overtime? They have to do so because they are paid by the piece and the rate is very low.'

Workers like these were unable to improve their conditions. Trade unions were not allowed by law. Going on strike was illegal. Anyway, employers could easily replace troublesome workers who complained: there were always long queues of unemployed people outside their factory gates looking for work.

The rich

Not all Russians were poor. Russian nobles were, for the most part, fabulously rich. Tsar Nicholas, at the head of the nobility, owned eight different palaces and employed 15,000 servants. When the royal family moved from one palace to another, up to twenty railway carriages were needed just for their luggage.

Although the nobles were only 1 per cent of the Russian population, they owned around 25 per cent of all the land. Those who could be bothered to farm their land efficiently made handsome profits at

A Russian cartoon of 1900. Above the workers are the capitalists: 'We do the eating'; then the army: 'We shoot you'; the clergy: 'We mislead you'; and the royal family: 'We rule you'

market. Those who could not be bothered were always able to sell off a little of their land to pay for their idle and luxurious lifestyles.

By 1900 a new class of Russians was also becoming rich – the **capitalists** who made money from banking, industry and trade. The Minister of Finance, Sergei Witte, made it easy for capitalists to make big profits. He gave them government contracts, particularly for building railways. He gave them loans to build new factories. He cut taxes. With easy profits to be made the capitalists did little to improve the conditions of their workers. Hatred of the capitalists steadily grew in the slums and boarding houses of Russia's cities.

Work section

A. Test your understanding of this chapter by explaining the meanings of the following words: serfdom, mir, redemption payments, capitalists.

B. Study the extract by Father Gapon, then answer these questions:
  1. a) What, according to Father Gapon, was the length of the working day allowed by law?
     b) How long did most workers actually work each day?
     c) For what reason did workers accept such long hours of work?
  2. Compare the photograph of a Moscow boarding house with this extract. In what ways does the photograph agree with Father Gapon's account of life in St Petersburg?

C. Study the cartoon above. Then, using the information in Chapter 2 as well as this chapter, explain what you think was the point of the cartoon. Judging by what you have read, do you think the cartoonist was being fair? Explain your answer.

OPPONENTS OF THE TSAR

An artist's view of the assassination of Tsar Alexander II, March 1881

Most Russians did not question the Tsar's autocratic system of government. They believed that God had appointed the Tsar to rule over them and that everyone else had their rightful place in society. But some people refused to accept this. They wanted to get rid of the Tsar and make big changes to Russian government and society. Some of them were ready to go to any lengths to achieve this.

Terrorism

On a snowy Sunday afternoon in March 1881 a bomb exploded beneath the carriage of Tsar Alexander II, the Tsar who had freed the peasants from serfdom twenty years earlier. He was unhurt, but when he got out of his carriage to inspect the damage, a young man stepped forward and threw what looked like a snowball at his feet. The snowball exploded, tearing off one of Alexander's legs and ripping his belly open. He bled to death shortly after, watched by his son Alexander and his grandson Nicholas.

The assassination of Alexander II was carried out by a terrorist group called the 'People's Will'. It was one of many small terrorist groups determined to destroy the autocracy by any means. But the assassination did not destroy the autocracy. Alexander's

successors, his son Alexander III and his grandson Nicholas II, who both watched him die, were determined not to let the same happen to them. Both used the Okhrana to arrest critics and opponents. Many thousands ended up in prison or in exile in Siberia.

Neither Alexander nor Nicholas succeeded in wiping out all their opponents, however. In 1900 there were still three important groups of opponents in existence.

The Socialist Revolutionary Party

The first of these groups was the Socialist Revolutionary Party. The SRs, as its members were known, wanted all land in Russia to be given to the mirs, the village communes, so that peasants could have a bigger share of the land. This would mean taking away land from the Tsar, the nobles and the church, who between them owned most of Russia.

To help achieve their aims the SRs had a 'Fighting Organisation' whose job was to organise terrorist campaigns. Between 1900 and 1905 the 'Fighting Organisation' managed to kill three government ministers and dozens of other government officials.

Not surprisingly the SRs gained support from millions of peasants who wanted their own land but who had fallen behind with their yearly redemption payments.

The Social Democratic Party

Another important revolutionary group in 1900 was the Social Democratic Party. The Social Democrats followed the ideas of **Karl Marx**, a German writer who in 1848 had written a book called the *Communist Manifesto*. In this book Marx predicted that there would be a violent revolution in which the working class overthrew the capitalists who owned the wealth of the country. The workers would take away factories, mines, machinery and raw materials from the capitalists and would share them out equally among themselves. Marx called this sharing of wealth **socialism**.

In a socialist society, Marx thought, people would learn to work together for the good of everyone, not just for themselves. They would stop being selfish and would take only what they needed as payment for their work. At this stage, a system of **communism** would come into existence, a society in which people work according to their abilities and are paid according to their needs.

The Social Democratic Party, which followed Marx's ideas, was set up in 1898. However, its leaders quickly began to argue about what was the best way to start a socialist revolution. In 1903 they split into two groups, the **Bolsheviks** and the **Mensheviks**.

The Bolsheviks believed that the revolution should be organised by a small group of dedicated and skilled revolutionaries. They should lead the party and make all the decisions. The Mensheviks believed that the Party should be a mass party with as many working class members as possible. It should be run democratically, with the members electing the leaders and deciding on its policies.

The leader of the Bolsheviks, **Vladimir Ilyich Lenin**, argued that if the Mensheviks had their way, it would take years to start the revolution: they would waste time on useless discussion and argument. Julius Martov, leader of the Mensheviks, replied that the revolution would fail if it did not have the support of the whole working class.

The Social Democratic Party remained split on this issue. Lenin and his supporters failed to reach agreement with Martov and his supporters. So from 1903 onwards there were three important revolutionary groups in Russia – the Bolsheviks, the Mensheviks, and the Socialist Revolutionaries.

Liberals

Not all the Tsar's opponents were violent revolutionaries. Many law-abiding Russians, particularly those who owned property, were liberals. They supported the Tsar but they wanted him to share his power. They wanted a democratic system of government, like the one in Britain where an elected parliament shared power with the monarch.

Sadly for the liberals, Alexander II had made plans for a Russian parliament the day before he was blown up by the 'People's Will'. The first thing his son Alexander III did when he became Tsar was to tear up those plans.

V. I. Lenin (centre) and J. Martov (sitting on Lenin's left) and members of the Union of Struggle for Liberation of the Working People, a revolutionary group set up in 1895

Work section

A. Study the information in this chapter about the assassination of Tsar Alexander II, then answer these questions:
1. Which terrorist group assassinated Alexander II? What was its aim in doing so?
2. In your opinion, was the assassination likely to achieve the aim of the assassins? Explain your answer.
3. How did the assassination ruin the liberals' chances of achieving their aims?

B. Study the photograph above. Then, using the information you have read in this chapter, answer these questions:
1. To which party did V.I. Lenin and J. Martov both belong?
2. On what did the two men agree and on what did they disagree?
3. V.I. Lenin's name was really V.I. Ulyanov, and J. Martov was really called I.O. Tserbaum. Why do you think both men changed their names?

5

THE 1905 REVOLUTION

War against Japan

In 1904 Russia went to war with Japan. They were fighting for control of Korea and Manchuria in the Far East (see map on page 3). Tsar Nicholas was glad to go to war. He thought that a quick victory would make him popular and would stop people criticising his government.

Right from the start of the war the Russian army suffered one terrible defeat after another. To help the army Nicholas sent the Russian Baltic fleet on a seven month voyage half way round the world to Manchuria. But as soon as the Russian fleet arrived in Japanese waters the Japanese fleet destroyed all but three of the Russian ships in the **battle of Tsushima**.

Far from making Nicholas popular, the war with Japan weakened his position. The war also made conditions for working people worse than before: food supplies to the cities broke down and factories closed as raw materials ran short. Workers found themselves out of work and out on the streets.

Bloody Sunday

On Sunday 22 January, 1905, a crowd of 200,000 workers and their families marched through the streets of St Petersburg towards the Tsar's Winter Palace. Their aim was to present Nicholas with a petition asking for better working and living conditions, an end to the war with Japan, a shorter working day, and many other reforms. The marchers were led by **Father Gapon**, a priest who sympathised with poor workers.

When the marchers reached the centre of St Petersburg, soldiers and police tried to stop them. Scuffles broke out and then the soldiers opened fire, aiming low. Around 500 marchers were killed and thousands more were wounded.

This dreadful massacre quickly came to be known as **Bloody Sunday**. As news of the massacre spread through Russia, there were riots in the countryside and strikes in the towns. Hundreds of government officials were murdered. Tsar Nicholas's uncle, the Grand Duke Serge, was blown to pieces by a terrorist bomb. Bloody Sunday had started a revolution against the Tsar.

The 1905 revolution

In June 1905 the crew of the battleship **Potemkin**, pride of the Black Sea fleet, threw their officers overboard and took control of the ship. This was mutiny. Although the mutineers had no plan, and gave them-

selves up only a few weeks later, the mutiny was very threatening to Tsar Nicholas. It showed that he could not trust his armed forces.

Just as worrying for Nicholas was the behaviour of peasants in the countryside. In many areas peasants had rebelled, butchering their landlords and burning their farms. At the same time, many of the non-Russian peoples of the Empire, peoples such as the Georgians and the Poles, took the opportunity to declare their independence from Russian rule.

Then in September 1905 a general strike began. All over Russia factories, offices, shops, railways, hospitals and schools closed down. In many towns and cities the strikers set up councils called **Soviets** to run the towns during the strike. The Soviets quickly became an alternative form of government, for the striking workers were willing to obey the orders of the Soviets, even though they would not obey the Tsar's government.

THE CZAR OF ALL THE RUSSIAS.

A British cartoon which appeared in Punch *magazine in February 1905. 'Czar' is an old-fashioned spelling of 'Tsar'*

A barricade put up by revolutionaries across a street in Moscow, December 1905

Faced with all these problems, Nicholas had to give way. In October 1905 he issued a document called the **October Manifesto**. This said that Russia could have a **Duma**, an elected parliament, to help run the country. It also allowed the Russian people basic rights, such as the right to form political parties and the right of free speech.

The liberals were delighted with the October Manifesto, but the revolutionary parties did not trust Nicholas to keep his word. They were proved right in December when the police arrested the members of the St Petersburg Soviet and sent fifteen of them into exile in Siberia. In Moscow an army was sent to crush the Soviet and more than a thousand people died in street fighting between revolutionaries and soldiers.

In the early months of 1906 the Tsar crushed all other areas of revolution. Worse, bands of thugs known as Black Hundreds decided to take the law into their own hands. They organised massacres of revolutionaries. In over 100 cities people who had joined in the revolution were put to death in blood-baths which the police and army did nothing to stop.

By March 1906 the revolution was over. But at least Russia had got a parliament out of it – the Duma. Elections for the Duma were held in March 1906 and a majority of anti-government candidates gained office. But when the Duma met for the first time in May, Nicholas issued a set of **Fundamental Laws**. The first one said 'To the Emperor of all the Russias belongs supreme autocratic power'. In other words, as far as Nicholas was concerned, nothing much had changed. Duma or no Duma, Russia was still an autocracy.

Work section

A. Make a time chart of the events of the 1905 revolution in Russia. You should be able to find eight important events in this chapter. Start in January 1905 and finish in March 1906.

Example:

1905 ⌐ January

                   22: Bloody Sunday. 500 demonstrators in St Petersburg shot dead by troops

     ⌐ February

B. Study the *Punch* cartoon opposite. Then, using the information you have read in this chapter, answer these questions:
   1. Who is the figure clutching a 'Petition' meant to be? Why is the figure shown lying on the ground?
   2. Who is the skeleton on the throne meant to be? Why do you think the cartoonist has drawn this person as a skeleton?
   3. Explain what message you think the cartoonist was trying to put across.
   4. Why would you have been unlikely to find a cartoon like this in a Russian newspaper or magazine in 1905?

C. Study the photograph above. What do you think the purpose of the barricade was?

11

6

THE AFTERMATH OF THE 1905 REVOLUTION

A session of the first Duma in June 1906

The Dumas

Tsar Nicholas made it perfectly clear in his Fundamental Laws that he would not allow the Duma, Russia's new parliament, any real power. Sure enough, when it demanded a share in government, Nicholas surrounded its meeting place with troops and broke it up. Russia's first Duma had lasted for precisely seventy-five days.

A second Duma was elected in 1907, but it was even less to Nicholas's liking. It contained not only liberals but also Socialist Revolutionaries and Social Democrats who aimed to destroy the autocracy. Nicholas broke up the second Duma after three months.

The third Duma, which met in 1907, did better than its two predecessors, lasting a full five years. This was because Nicholas changed the voting laws to make sure that revolutionaries were not elected to it. The third Duma was mostly made up of conservative politicians who behaved themselves and did what Nicholas wanted.

With the powerless third Duma providing a show of democracy, Nicholas got on with the business of autocracy. In 1906 he appointed a new, tough Prime Minister to make sure there were no more outbreaks of revolution. His name was **Peter Stolypin**.

The Stolypin reforms

Stolypin believed in strict government. His first action as Prime Minister was to clamp down on terrorism. In 1906 1008 terrorists were arrested, tried by special military courts, and executed. (Russians gave the gallows a new nickname in 1906: 'Stolypin's Necktie'.) In the same year 21,000 people were exiled to Siberia. Before long terrorism had ceased to be a serious threat to the autocracy.

Stolypin realised that brute force alone would not solve every problem. He feared that there would be further outbreaks of violence in the countryside if the peasants remained poor. Stolypin therefore helped the peasants to become the owners of their own land. The redemption payments that peasants had been paying since 1861 were abolished. So too was the law which said that the village communes, the mirs, controlled the land. Stolypin hoped that hardworking peasants would now leave the communes and set up their own farms. These farms would be bigger and more productive that the communal farms. In time, he thought, the peasants who owned land would grow rich. They would want peace in the countryside and would therefore help to prevent revolution.

Conditions in Russia began to improve. Industry grew, wages increased and the harvests were good. Millions of peasants bought their own land and set about creating new, efficient farms. In 1911, however, one of Stolypin's police agents who had been investigating terrorist groups turned out to be a terrorist himself: he shot Stolypin dead.

Rasputin

While Stolypin was Prime Minister, Nicholas and his wife Alexandra became involved with a strange Siberian peasant who claimed to be a *Starets* – a holy man of God.

As you read in Chapter 2, Nicholas and Alexandra were both very religious. When they found out that their only son, Alexis, had the incurable disease haemophilia, Alexandra began to pray daily for his recovery. In 1905 it seemed as if her prayers had been answered. Two ladies of the court introduced Nicholas and Alexandra to a man whom they said had special powers of prophecy and healing. His name was Gregory Efimovitch. Shortly after this Alexis had a fall which started off internal bleeding. Gregory Efimovitch prayed at Alexis's bedside and the next morning Alexis had fully recovered. Nicholas and Alexandra were amazed and delighted at what they thought was a miracle. From then on the *Starets* was one of the most trusted members of their court.

Gregory Efimovitch was not regarded with such favour by everyone. Years before, people in his native Siberia had given him the nickname **Rasputin** – the disreputable one – because he drank heavily and had affairs with many local women. At court in St Petersburg he proved to be more than 'disreputable'. He took part in wild orgies, he spent much of his time drunk, and he once raped a nun. But whenever Nicholas and Alexandra were told about Rasputin's wild behaviour, they refused to listen, and continued to put all their trust in him.

After the death of Stolypin in 1911 Rasputin's influence over the royal family increased. He began to give political advice to Alexandra which she passed on to Nicholas. Ambitious politicians now found it easier to gain promotion if they were friendly with Rasputin. Businessmen who entertained Rasputin seemed to get government contracts more easily than those who didn't.

As Rasputin's influence increased, hatred of him grew. Rumours began to go around that he was having an affair with Alexandra. He was discussed by the Duma, and the newspapers were full of gossip about him. It seemed as if all Russia knew about Rasputin's corruption – all except the 'Supreme Autocrat' and his wife.

Gregory Rasputin (centre) with two of the Tsar's military advisers

Work section

A. Test your understanding of this chapter by explaining the following terms: the Fundamental Laws, Duma, 'Stolypin's Necktie', *Starets*, Rasputin.

B. Study the photograph above. Then, using the information in this chapter, answer these questions:
1. Why do you think the two advisers of the Tsar posed for this photograph with Gregory Rasputin?
2. Why do you think Rasputin was willing to pose for this photograph?
3. Why might the two advisers of the Tsar be called unwise for posing for this photograph with Rasputin? Explain your answer.

C. Make revision notes on what you have read in Chapters 3 to 6. If you are unsure about how to organise your notes, use points C to F of the revision guide on the next page.

Revision guide

These revision notes may either be copied or used as a framework for your own notes. If you decide to copy them you will have to fill in the blank words.

A. The Russian Empire in 1900

1. Russia is very big but much of it is too cold to be useful. In the Arctic Circle the land is t. . . .a where little grows. South of this is the t. . .a, or pine forest. Only in the south is the land warm enough for farming.
2. In 1900 the cold also affected trade because much of the coastline was frozen for half the year and there were few ice breakers. However, the T. . .s-S. . . . . .n Railway was being built to improve trade between east and west.
3. The Russian Empire contained many peoples, the majority of them non-Russian – e.g. 22 million U. . . . . . .s in the south and 8 million P. . .s in the west. Many of these peoples disliked Russian rule and wanted i. . . . . .e.

B. The government of Russia

1. The head of the government was T. . . N. . . . . . II. He ruled as an a. . . . . .t, a ruler who does not have to share power.
2. The work of the government was done by a large and corrupt c. . .l s. . . . .e. Opponents of the Tsar were dealt with by a political police force, the O. . . . .a. Rebellions and riots were put down by the C. . . . . .s.
3. The church in Russia, the O. . . . . .x Church, supported the government by encouraging Russians to be loyal to the Tsar and to respect authority.

C. Russian society

1. Peasants in Russia had been s. . .s until 1861 when Tsar A. . . . . .r freed them. At the same time as being freed, peasants had their farming land put under the control of their village communes, the m. .s. Peasants who wanted to buy the land they farmed had to pay for it in forty-nine instalments over the next fifty years. Life therefore remained hard for the peasants even after they had been freed.
2. The number of workers in towns was increasing in 1900. The largest city was the capital, S. P. . . . . . .g, with over 1 million inhabitants. They worked long hours, lived in slums, and were not allowed to join t. . .e u. . . .s or to strike.
3. The richest people were n. . . .s who, along with the Tsar and the Church, owned most of the land. A new class of c. . . . . . . .s, businessmen and industrialists, was also growing rich as the government gave help to industry in the 1890s and 1900s.

D. The opponents of the Tsar

1. Some opponents used terrorism to try to destroy the autocracy, e.g. the P. . . . .s W. .l killed Alexander II in 1881.
2. Most of the Tsar's opponents belonged to two parties which wanted revolution. One was the S. . . . . .t R. . . . . .y Party which wanted the peasants to own all land. The other was the Social Democratic Party which followed the ideas of K. .l M. .x and wanted a communist society.
3. In 1903 the Social Democrats split into two groups, the B. . . . . . .s led by Lenin and the M. . . . . . .s led by Martov.
4. Other opponents of the Tsar included liberals who wanted a British style of democracy, with the Tsar sharing power with an elected p. . . . . . .t.

E. The 1905 revolution

1. Russia was defeated in a war against J. . .n in 1904–5. The war caused food shortages and unemployment.
2. In January 1905 troops fired on an anti-war demonstration in St Petersburg, killing 500 people. This massacre, known as B. . . .y S. . . .y, triggered off a revolution.
3. In June 1905 there was a mutiny on the battleship P. . . . . .n. There were peasant riots and many non-Russian peoples of the Empire declared i. . . . . .e.
4. A g. . . . .l s. . . .e began in October 1905. Councils of workers called S. . . . .s were set up to run the strike.
5. In October Tsar Nicholas issued the O. . . . .r M. . . . . . .o, promising a Duma.
6. In December the Tsar crushed the revolution with the help of the army and bands of thugs called B. . .k H. . . . . .s.
7. When the first Duma met in 1906 Nicholas issued F. . . . . .l L. .s, showing that he intended to continue ruling as an autocrat.

F. The Stolypin years, 1906–11

1. Nicholas got rid of the first two Dumas when they demanded more power. A third, tame Duma continued to meet for five years.
2. A new Prime Minister, S. . . . . . ., clamped down on terrorism. He also made it easier for peasants to buy their own land. He thought this would stop them from wanting a revolution.
3. From 1905 onwards Nicholas and Alexandra were under the influence of R. . . . . .n who seemed to be able to stop their son's attacks of bleeding. However, his wild behaviour and his corruption gave Nicholas and Alexandra a bad name.

WAR AND REVOLUTION

Cossacks demonstrating against the Tsar in Petrograd (the new name for St Petersburg) in March 1917

Think carefully about the scene in the photograph above – Cossacks demonstrating against the monarchy in the streets of the capital.

You have come across the Cossacks before, charging with sabres drawn against striking workers or rebellious peasants (see pages 4–5). For two centuries the Cossacks had been the strong arm of the autocracy, defenders of the Tsars and all they stood for. Now, in March 1917, their sabres are drawn not against workers or peasants, but against the Tsar. What has gone wrong? Why can the 'Supreme Autocrat' no longer rely on his old defenders?

You will find out in Part Two of this book that the problem was all to do with another war. Russia went to war in 1914 to fight Germany and Austria. Like most people in 1914, Russian soldiers believed they were going to fight a short, exciting war, and that they would be home for Christmas. They were very wrong. The 'short war' grew into the Great War of 1914–18, killing millions of people from fifty different countries and wrecking Europe.

The last time Russia had gone to war was in 1904–5, against Japan. The result had been defeat for the Russian army and misery for the people at home. Exactly the same thing happened between 1914 and 1917. And just as war led to revolution in 1905, so the Great War led to revolution again in 1917. The difference was that, this time, there were two revolutions in the space of a year, and that Tsar Nicholas and his family ended up dead.

15

7

RUSSIA AT WAR, 1914–17

Russia went to war in August 1914. The news that the country was at war was very popular. All over Russia there were patriotic demonstrations in support of the Tsar. Hatred of Germany spread like wildfire. Nicholas renamed St Petersburg, which he thought sounded too much like a German name, Petrograd.

Early defeats

Two huge Russian armies attacked Germany at the end of August 1914. They should have won a great victory against the single German army facing them. But the Russian armies were badly led and badly equipped: nearly a million men were without rifles, and many didn't even have boots. In two battles, at **Tannenberg** and the **Masurian Lakes**, both Russian armies were wiped out. Over 250,000 Russian soldiers were killed, wounded or taken prisoner. And this was only six weeks after the start of the war. By the end of 1914 the Russians had lost over one million men through casualties, deaths and soldiers taken prisoner.

The collapse of the economy

As the war continued in 1915 the Russian economy began to collapse. The first problem was a lack of workers. In all, 15.5 million young men were taken into the armies to fight, halving the number needed to work in the factories and the fields. In 1915 nearly 600 factories had to close because they didn't have enough workers. On many farms weeds grew in empty fields where corn had once grown.

The next problem was transport. Russia, the biggest country in the world, depended on railways for food and raw materials. But there were not enough trains to keep the armies as well as the towns-people supplied with food and materials. Thousands of tonnes of butter, meat and grain rotted in railway sidings in the countryside, while soldiers and people in the towns went hungry, simply because there weren't enough trains to transport them. Coal supplies to factories and power stations halted while coal trains stood at the coal mines waiting for engines to pull them. And as the power failed, so more factories had to close.

A third problem was inflation. Russian money, the rouble, began to lose its value in 1914. At the same time food prices went up. People therefore found that their wages were buying less and less food.

Meanwhile, on the fighting fronts, defeat followed defeat. By the end of 1915 300,000 Russians had been killed and three million were either wounded or locked up in enemy prison camps.

'Dark forces destroying the throne'

In August 1915 Tsar Nicholas decided to take personal command of his armies. He left Petrograd and went to live at army headquarters, 500 kilometres

A Russian painting of September 1914 shows soldiers kneeling in prayer as Tsar Nicholas blesses them. He is holding up an icon, or holy picture

Russian lands lost to Germany and Austria 1914–17

Russian forces retreat after being beaten by the Austrian army in Galicia, Austria, 1916

away. This was a fatal mistake, for he left Alexandra in charge of the government in Petrograd – and she was by now completely under the influence of Rasputin.

For the next sixteen months – from August 1915 to the end of 1916 – Alexandra was able to do more or less what she liked. She used her power to sack ministers who displeased her and replace them with men whom she, and Rasputin, favoured. During these sixteen months Russia had four different Prime Ministers, five Ministers of the Interior, four Ministers of Agriculture, three Ministers of War and two Ministers of Foreign Affairs.

With ministers coming and going at such speed, the work of the government ground to a halt. Food, fuel and ammunition were already in short supply,

but now they became almost unobtainable. And although the Russian armies won some important victories in 1916, the death toll of Russian soldiers continued to rocket until it went over one million.

In Petrograd ugly rumours about Alexandra and Rasputin flew around. People were well aware that Alexandra was German by birth, and now they put two and two together to explain Russia's defeats: Alexandra and Rasputin were German agents, working to destroy Russia from within! Even the closest supporters of the Tsar were in despair. One of them spoke out in the Duma, saying that there were 'dark forces destroying the throne'. In December 1916 three nobles loyal to the Tsar decided to destroy those 'dark forces'. They murdered Rasputin.

When the news of Rasputin's death was announced there was public rejoicing. People kissed each other in the streets when they heard that the 'dark forces' were no more. But Rasputin's death did not help Russia. The new year, 1917, began with blizzards and temperatures as low as 35°C below zero. More than a thousand railway engines froze and burst their boilers. Supplies of grain, coal, wood and oil dwindled to nothing. As people huddled freezing in their homes, conditions became right for revolution.

Work section

A. Using the information you have read in this chapter, as well as the map above, explain how the Great War affected:

1. Russia's land
2. Russian industry
3. Russia's transport system
4. Russian soldiers
5. The rouble
6. The Russian government.

B. Study the painting opposite of Tsar Nicholas blessing his troops. Now answer these questions:

1. In your opinion, what image of Tsar Nicholas was the artist trying to give?
2. What picture of the state of the army in 1914 does this painting give?
3. Compare the painting with the photograph on this page. In what ways does the photograph give a different picture of the Russian army?
4. In your opinion, which gives the more realistic view: the painting or the photograph? Explain your answer.

8

THE REVOLUTION OF MARCH 1917

Soldiers and workers together behind a barricade in a Petrograd street, March 1917

During the month of March 1917 conditions in Russia grew rapidly worse. In the capital, Petrograd, discontent turned into a full-scale revolution which overthrew the Tsar. This is how it happened:

Wednesday 7 March
The managers of the giant Putilov steel works locked out their 20,000 workers after pay talks broke down. This meant that 20,000 tough, angry steel workers were now out on the streets in a mood for trouble. Workers in other factories went on strike in support of the steel workers.

Thursday 8 March
Fifty factories closed down and 90,000 workers went out on strike. As this was International Women's Day there were also thousands of socialist women on the streets, demonstrating. The subject on everybody's mind was bread, as Sybil Grey, an Englishwoman living in Petrograd, recorded in her diary:

A. 'On Thursday March 8th a poor woman entered a bread shop on the Morskaia [*a shopping street in Petrograd*] and asked for bread. She was told there was none. On leaving the shop, seeing bread in the window, she broke the window and took it. A general, passing in his motor, stopped and remonstrated with her [*told her off*]. A crowd collected round them, smashed his motor car, and increasing in size, paraded the streets asking for bread.'

Friday 9 March
200,000 workers were on strike. According to Leon Trotsky, writing in his *History of the Russian Revolution* in 1932,

B. 'About one half of the industrial workers of Petrograd are on strike . . . The workers come to the factories in the mornings; instead of going to work, they hold meetings; then begin the processions towards the centre . . .

Throughout the entire day, crowds of people poured from one part of the city to the other. They were persistently dispelled by the police, stopped and crowded back by cavalry detachments and occasionally by the infantry.'

Saturday 10 March

250,000 workers were on strike. There was no public transport and no newspapers. Food shortages continued. Louis de Robien, a French diplomat living in Petrograd, wrote in his diary:

C. 'The movement has taken on a political character . . . In the square in front of the Kazan Cathedral there are reserves of infantry . . . The troops opened fire in the Nevsky Prospekt [*Petrograd's main street*] at about six o'clock . . . Most of the rounds were blank . . . All the same there were some killed and wounded.'

Later in the day, Cossacks refused to attack a procession of strikers when they were ordered to do so.

Sunday 11 March

The President of the Duma, Michael Rodzianko, sent this telegram to the Tsar:

D. 'The situation is serious. The capital is in a state of anarchy. The government is paralysed; the transport system is broken down; the food and fuel supplies are completely disorganised. Discontent is general and on the increase. There is wild shooting on the streets; troops are firing at each other. It is urgent that someone enjoying the confidence of the country be entrusted with the formation of a new government.'

The Tsar's response to this telegram was to order the Duma to stop meeting.

Monday 12 March

At six o'clock in the morning a mutiny began in the Volinsky regiment of the army: a sergeant shot his commanding officer dead. The soldiers then left their barracks and marched into the centre of Petrograd. Louis de Robien recorded the results in his diary:

E. 'Serious mutiny has broken out among the troops and all the men we saw belong to regiments sent to restore order, who, after firing a few volleys, made common cause with the mutineers. All the units sent to fight the mutiny are defecting [*changing sides*] one after another.'

Later in the day the Duma held a meeting, despite the Tsar's order not to do so. It set up a twelve-man committee called the **Provisional Committee** to take over the government.

That evening, revolutionaries set up a **Soviet**, or council, of workers and soldiers in Petrograd. The Petrograd Soviet also intended to take over the government and immediately began to organise food supplies for the city.

Tuesday 13 March

Tsar Nicholas sent a telegram to the Duma, saying that he would share power with the Duma. Michael Rodzianko, the Duma leader, replied:

F. 'The measures you propose are too late. The time for them has gone. There is no return.'

Wednesday 14 March

Leading army generals sent telegrams to Nicholas, informing him that none of the army supported him. Nicholas, 500 km away in army headquarters, now tried to return to Petrograd to take control of the situation. But, according to Louis de Robien:

G. 'My first impression on leaving the house this morning was a better one. There seem to be fewer shots and there is some attempt at organisation: in fact, I met a convoy of sledges carrying food supplies, escorted by soldiers . . . It is said that the Emperor has left Headquarters, but that his train has been stopped by the revolutionaries while he was on his way to Tsarskoe Selo [*a royal palace near Petrograd*].'

Thursday 15 March

Nicholas, now 250 km away from Petrograd where revolutionaries had halted his train, agreed to abdicate and give the throne to Alexis. Later he realised that Alexis was too ill to be Tsar and gave the crown to his brother, Grand Duke Michael, instead.

Grand Duke Michael, however, feared that he would be just as unpopular as Nicholas, and within twenty-four hours he too had abdicated. Russia was now a republic – a country governed not by a monarch but by an elected leader. The question was, which elected body should govern Russia – the Duma's Provisional Committee or the Petrograd Soviet?

Work section

Study sources A–G in this chapter, then answer these questions:
1. What were the two main forms of protest taking place in Petrograd on 7, 8 and 9 March?
2. According to source C, how did the situation in Petrograd change on Saturday 10 March?
3. In source D, what do you think Michael Rodzianko meant by 'The capital is in a state of anarchy'?
4. Why, according to source E, was it impossible to stop the mutiny in the army from spreading?
5. Why do you think Michael Rodzianko told the Tsar (source F) that it was too late to share his power with the Duma?
6. What, in extract G, suggests that the Petrograd Soviet was gaining control of the situation in Petrograd?

9

THE PROVISIONAL GOVERNMENT

Two new governments

Russia's new government was the twelve-man committee that the Duma had set up on 12 March. The twelve men called themselves the **Provisional Government**, meaning that they would govern Russia for a short time until elections could be held. Then they would resign.

The Provisional Government was the official government. But across the corridor from their meeting place in the Tauride Palace was a second, unofficial government, the **Petrograd Soviet** of Workers' and Soldiers' Deputies. This council, which had been elected by working people, aimed to protect the interests of working people and soldiers. Other Soviets with the same aim were formed in towns all over Russia during March, and they all took their lead from the Petrograd Soviet. Whatever the Petrograd Soviet decided was imitated by the other soviets. This gave it great power.

The first action of the Petrograd Soviet was to issue an order to the armed forces. **Order No. 1** said that soldiers and sailors must set up committees to take control of all arms, ammunition and equipment. Off-duty soldiers were not to salute their officers and had to address them as 'Mister Colonel', 'Mister General',

and so on, instead of 'Your Excellency'. Order No. 1 was obeyed in all parts of the army and navy, showing that the Petrograd Soviet, not the Provisional Government, controlled the armed forces.

Many of the 2500 deputies in the Petrograd Soviet were revolutionaries, especially SRs and Mensheviks. There were also some Bolsheviks. As you know, the revolutionary parties wanted all land to be given to the peasants, and factories to be given to the workers. But most of the revolutionaries in the Soviet did not want to push their demands too far. For the time being they were willing to co-operate with the Provisional Government, and to wait for the changes they wanted.

Lenin and the April Theses

At the time of the March Revolution the leader of the Bolsheviks, Lenin, was in exile in Switzerland. He disagreed with the revolutionaries who co-operated with the Provisional Government. He wanted to get back to Russia to organise a second revolution.

Petrograd, however, was 2000 km away and the lands between Switzerland and Russia were held by Germany and Austria, Russia's enemies in the Great

The July Days: a crowd in Petrograd scatters to escape bullets fired by government troops

20

War. But the Germans were happy to help Lenin get back home. They knew he would make trouble for the Provisional Government, and that would help Germany in the war. So they provided Lenin with food, money and a special train in which he crossed Germany safely.

Lenin reached Petrograd on 16 April 1917. Soon after his arrival he made a speech to the Bolsheviks. There must be an end to the war with Germany, he said. All land must be given to the peasants. Banks must be nationalised. The Bolsheviks should change their name to 'Communists'. Lenin also said 'No support must be given to the Provisional Government'. Instead, the Soviets should get together to form a new government. 'All power to the Soviets!' Lenin said. These ideas later became known as the **April Theses**.

The April Theses were a great surprise to the Bolsheviks. Lenin was telling them to start a second revolution, but many of them thought that the time was not yet right. Before long their doubts were proved to be correct. In June 1917 the Russian armies made a major attack on Austria. The attack failed and turned into a retreat. Soldiers deserted from the armies in large numbers. Many went to Petrograd where they joined up with Bolsheviks to demand an end to the Provisional Government. More than 100,000 soldiers and Bolsheviks roamed the streets shouting 'All Power to the Soviets!' and demanding that the Bolsheviks should seize power.

After three days of rioting – the **July Days** – Alexander Kerensky, the Minister of War, sent loyal troops into Petrograd. On 16 and 17 July these troops broke up the mobs, killing and wounding 400 of them. Kerensky then claimed that the Bolsheviks had been paid by the Germans to make trouble, and that Lenin was a German agent. While Kerensky issued orders for his arrest, Lenin fled across the border into nearby Finland, in exile again. Other leading Bolsheviks were arrested and put in prison.

The Kornilov Revolt

Alexander Kerensky now became the Prime Minister of the Provisional Government. Immediately he was faced with a challenge from the Commander-in-Chief of the armies, General Kornilov. Kornilov believed that Russia needed a 'strong man' and that he himself should be in charge. He therefore planned to get rid

The Petrograd Soviet, June 1917

of the Petrograd Soviet, to arrest revolutionaries, and to take control of the Provisional Government so that he could get on with fighting Germany without interference.

Kornilov's rebel troops were some of the best in Russia – the Savage Division from the Caucasus mountains, and the Cossacks. Kornilov sent them to Petrograd with orders to get rid of the Provisional Government. Kerensky had few loyal troops to defend him, and it seemed as if Kornilov's revolt would succeed.

To help him defend Petrograd, Kerensky allowed the Bolsheviks to set up a defence force called the **Red Guards**. Within a few days 25,000 Bolsheviks armed with rifles and machine guns were out on the streets. Kornilov's troops refused to fight against fellow workers and Kornilov was soon arrested.

The Bolsheviks came out of the Kornilov revolt as heroes. They had saved the Provisional Government. This showed that they were not German agents after all. They also came out of it as an armed and disciplined fighting force. They strengthened their position even further when they got a majority in elections for the Petrograd Soviet in September. The same happened in elections for the Soviets of Moscow and other big cities.

By October 1917 the Bolsheviks were more powerful than they had ever been before. Again they began to consider carrying out a second revolution, and this time the chances of success looked good.

Work section

A. Test your understanding of this chapter by explaining the following words and terms: Provisional Government, Petrograd Soviet, Order No. 1, the April Theses, Red Guards.

B. Study the photograph opposite, then answer these questions:
1. Judging by what you have read about the July Days in this chapter, what do you think the people in the photograph were doing before the shooting started?
2. What kinds of people do you think they were, and which political party do you think they supported?
3. Why did the party they supported fail to take power in July 1917?

10

THE BOLSHEVIK REVOLUTION OF NOVEMBER 1917

During September and October 1917 Kerensky and the Provisional Government gradually lost their authority. Peasants in the countryside rebelled, soldiers in the army refused to fight the Germans, and Bolshevik workers in the cities got ready for a second revolution.

The state of Russia in September 1917

During the summer of 1917 peasants began to take control of the land on which they grew their food. They had been waiting since March for the Provisional Government to give them land, but it had failed to do so. On more than 2000 farms peasants killed their landlords and divided the land up among themselves. In other areas they seized the lands of the Church and the Tsar.

Kerensky tried to stop the peasants from grabbing land by sending soldiers on 'punishment expeditions' into the countryside. Several expeditions went out, whipping peasants and burning their homes. But Kerensky could not find enough loyal troops to do this dirty work for him, so in most areas the violence between landlords and peasants continued.

The violence in the countryside delayed the harvest on many farms, and this led to food shortages. As you know, Russia was already desperately short of food, so now people faced the winter with the threat of famine.

In the armies discipline was breaking down. The Petrograd Soviet's Order No. 1 in March had already led many soldiers to disobey orders given by their officers. Now, thousands of soldiers were deserting from the army every week, mostly to go back to their villages to make sure they got their fair share of land. In the front lines Bolsheviks encouraged soldiers to lay down their weapons and to give up fighting. Everywhere in the army there was drunkenness, chaos and violence. In many parts of the front line soldiers amused themselves by rolling live hand grenades into their officers' quarters. In October the Army General Headquarters admitted in a report that

> 'The army is simply a huge, weary, shabby and ill-fed mob of angry men united by their common thirst for peace and by common disappointment.'

The November Revolution

In October 1917 Lenin returned to Petrograd from his hiding place in Finland. At a Bolshevik meeting he said that they should begin a revolution immediately. He said:

> 'Hunger does not wait. The peasant uprising does not wait. The war does not wait.'

The Bolshevik leaders agreed to stage an armed uprising against the Provisional Government. Leon Trotsky, the Bolshevik chairman of the Petrograd Soviet, drew up the plans and set up headquarters in the **Smolny Institute**, a disused school.

Trotsky did not have to make his plans in secret because there was nothing Kerensky and the Provisional Government could do to stop him. The

Soldiers of the Women's Battalion on parade outside the Winter Palace in 1917

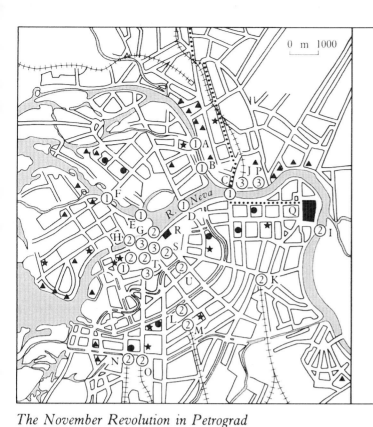

The legend of the map reads:

● Garrisons loyal to Provisional Government

★ Garrisons which supported the Bolsheviks

▲ Factories which were pro-Bolshevik and anti-war

.... Lenin's route on 6 November: HQ at Smolny Institute

① Night of 6 November: first objectives, including main bridges and telegraph station, seized

② Day of 7 November: second objectives, including railway stations, seized

③ Evening of 7 November: third objectives, including Winter Palace (HQ of Provisional Government) seized

A	Grenaderskii Bridge
B	Sampsonievskii Bridge
C	Puteinyi Bridge
D	Troitskii Bridge
E	Birzhevoi Bridge
F	Tuchkov Bridge
G	Dvortsovyi Bridge
H	Nicholas Bridge
I	Okhtenskii Bridge
J	Finland Station
K	Nicholas Station
L	Electrical Station
M	Tsarskoye Selo Station
N	Baltic Station
O	Warsaw Station
P	Prison
Q	Smolny Institute
R	Winter Palace
S	Telegraph Station
T	Head Post Office
U	State Bank

The November Revolution in Petrograd

army said it would support the Bolsheviks, and the guards of the Peter and Paul Fortress gave all the rifles in the fortress to the Bolsheviks.

By the night of 6 November the Red Guards were well armed with the rifles from the Peter and Paul Fortress, and they were ready for action. During the night they began to take control of all the most important locations in Petrograd. You can see where they were on the map above. First they took control of six bridges across the river Neva. Then, in the morning of 7 November, they seized government buildings, the power station and the railway stations.

The Provisional Government had its headquarters in the **Winter Palace** and was guarded only by army cadets and the Women's Battalion of the army. In the evening of 7 November a cruiser, the **Aurora**, which Bolshevik sailors had captured, sailed up the river Neva and fired blank shells at the Winter Palace. Later the guns in the Peter and Paul fortress also opened fire on the Palace. Then the Red Guards stormed the Winter Palace. The Cadets and the Women's Battalion gave in without a fight. The ministers of the Provisional Government surrendered and were taken away under arrest.

The Bolsheviks now controlled Petrograd, the capital of Russia. The next day Lenin announced that he was setting up a new government. The Bolsheviks had come to power after a single day of rebellion in which eighteen people had been arrested and two people had been killed.

Work section

A. Study the photograph opposite, then answer these questions:
1. Why do you think the Provisional Government in the Winter Palace was defended only by Cadets and the Women's Battalion of the army?
2. How well trained and how well equipped do the soldiers in the Women's Battalion appear to be? Explain your answer.
3. Judging by what you have read in this chapter, why do you think the Cadets and the Women's Battalion gave in to the Red Guards without a fight?

B. Study the map of Petrograd above, then answer these questions:
1. What are locations A to I on the map? Why do you think the Bolsheviks began their uprising by seizing these locations?
2. What are locations J to O on the map? Why do you think the Bolsheviks seized these locations as the second stage of their uprising?
3. Why do you think the Bolsheviks seized locations S, T and U?

C. Make revision notes on the events of 1917, using the revision guide on the next page if you are unsure about how to organise your notes.

Revision guide

These note headings and sub-headings are designed as a framework for notes which you make for yourself from Chapters 7 to 10. They are not a complete set of notes to be copied. They follow on from the notes you have already made on Chapters 1 to 6.

G. Russia at war, 1914–17
1. Russian defeats in 1914
2. The collapse of the economy
   a) Lack of workers
   b) Transport problems
   c) Food and fuel shortages
   d) Inflation
3. Alexandra, Rasputin and the Russian government, 1915–16

H. The Revolution of March 1917
1. Strikes and food shortages
2. Mutinies in the army
3. The Duma's Provisional Committee
4. The formation of the Petrograd Soviet
5. The abdication of the Tsar

I. The Provisional Government
1. The Provisional Government and the Petrograd Soviet
2. Order No. 1 of the Petrograd Soviet
3. The return of Lenin to Russia
4. Lenin's April Theses
5. The July Days
6. The Kornilov Revolt
7. The position of the Bolsheviks in September 1917

J. The Bolshevik Revolution of November 1917
1. The state of Russia in summer 1917
   a) Violence in the countryside
   b) Food shortages
   c) The breakdown of the Russian army
2. The November Revolution
   a) Events
   b) Results

Revision exercise

This photograph is a still from a Russian film called *Ten Days that Shook the World*, made in 1927 by Sergei Eisenstein. It shows the storming of the Winter Palace by Red Guards. Study the scene and then answer the questions beneath.

1. How many people were killed in Petrograd during the Bolshevik seizure of power?
2. In the scene above, what impression of the fighting do you think the film director was trying to give?
3. Judging by what you have read about the storming of the Winter Palace, how accurate do you think this film reconstruction was? Explain your answer.
4. Do you think the Bolsheviks would have approved or disapproved of this view of the seizure of power? Explain your answer.

PART THREE
LENIN'S RUSSIA

Lenin in his office in 1918

The government which Lenin set up in November 1917 was called **Sovnarkom**, short for Council of Peoples Commissars. During the next few weeks, Soviets all over Russia joined in the revolution and took control of most towns and cities. By the end of 1917 nearly all Russia was in Soviet hands.

This did not mean, however, that Lenin and the Bolsheviks ruled Russia. Only fourteen out of twenty-five members of Sovnarkom were Bolsheviks. Not all the Soviets were run by Bolsheviks. And in the countryside most peasants supported the Socialist Revolutionaries, the rivals of the Bolsheviks.

Even more awkward from Lenin's point of view, the Provisional Government had arranged for elections to be held in November for a new kind of parliament, called the Constituent Assembly. It seemed certain that the Socialist Revolutionaries would win more votes than the Bolsheviks. If that happened the Bolsheviks would have to hand over control of Sovnarkom to their rivals.

And on top of all these problems Lenin had to carry out the promises he had made in the April Theses before the Revolution – to end the war against Germany, to provide the people with food, and to give land to the peasants. How could he do all that when he had no real control of the country?

Part Three of this book shows how Lenin did what seemed impossible – gained full control of Russia *and* carried out his promises. It also showed that the Russian people paid a high price for these things. It is for you to decide whether or not the price was worth paying.

11

'PEACE AT ANY PRICE'

The first decrees of Sovnarkom

Sovnarkom, with Lenin as chairman, began issuing decrees, or orders, on the day it was created. These decrees made great changes to Russia and to the Russian people:

8 November 1917 – a decree on land took 540 million acres of land away from the Tsar, the nobles, the church and other landlords. This land, six times the size of the British Isles, was given to the peasants to divide among themselves.

8 November – a decree on peace stated that Sovnarkom intended to make peace with Russia's enemies at once.

12 November – a decree on work established an eight-hour day and a forty-eight hour week for all industrial workers, and laid down rules about overtime and holidays.

14 November – a decree on unemployment insurance promised to give insurance to all workers against injury, illness and unemployment.

1 December – a decree on the press banned all non-Bolshevik newspapers.

11 December – Sovnarkom banned Russia's main liberal party, the Constitutional Democratic Party, and ordered the arrest of its leaders.

20 December – Lenin set up a political police force, the 'All-Russian Extraordinary Commission to fight Counter-Revolution and Espionage' – otherwise known as the **Cheka**. Its job was to deal with opponents and enemies of the Bolsheviks.

27 December – a decree on workers' control put all factories under the control of elected committees of workers.

27 December – a decree on banking put all banks in Russia under Sovnarkom's control.

31 December – a decree on marriage allowed couples to have non-religious weddings and made it easier to get a divorce.

The Constituent Assembly

In November 1917 elections were held for Russia's new parliament, the Constituent Assembly. They were the first free elections in Russian history.

You can easily see from the figures in the table of results on the next page that the Bolsheviks were badly

Two of the 'People's Commissars' – Lenin and Trotsky (standing on the right of the platform), Moscow 1917

beaten in the election. The Socialist Revolutionaries gained more seats in the Assembly than all the other parties put together.

Number of seats in the Constituent Assembly

Socialist Revolutionaries	370
Bolsheviks	175
Left wing Socialist Revolutionaries	40
Constitutional Democrats	17
Mensheviks	16
Narodniks	2
Others (representing nationalities)	87
Total	707

The Constituent Assembly met for the first time on 18 January 1918. Less than twenty-four hours later Sovnarkom ordered it to stop meeting. Bolshevik Red Guards with machine guns killed and wounded more than a hundred people who demonstrated in support of the Assembly outside its meeting place. The Red Guards then prevented the elected Deputies from entering the Assembly and closed it down permanently.

The Treaty of Brest-Litovsk

Lenin believed that a quick end to the war against Germany and Austria was needed if the Bolsheviks were to stay in power. Otherwise they would lose the support of the army. On 3 December 1917 a peace conference between Russia, Germany and Austria-Hungary began at Brest-Litovsk, a town on the border with Germany.

Leon Trotsky was Russia's Commissar, or minister, for Foreign Affairs. At the peace conference he dragged out the talks for as long as he could, hoping that a socialist revolution would begin in Germany. With a socialist government in Germany as well as Russia, he thought, the two countries could make a fair and democratic peace with each other.

Trotsky span out the talks for nine weeks but no revolution began in Germany. In February 1918 the German army advanced into Russia and got so close to Petrograd that Lenin decided to make peace at any price.

The Treaty of Brest-Litovsk between Russia and Germany was one of the harshest treaties ever made. As you can see from the map below, Russia had to give up all her western lands – Finland, Estonia, Latvia, Lithuania, Poland, the Ukraine and Georgia. These were the richest areas of the country, so Russia lost:

- sixty-two million people – 26 per cent of her population
- 27 per cent of her farm land
- 26 per cent of her railways
- 74 per cent of her iron ore and coal.

Russia also had to pay a fine of 300 million gold roubles to Germany.

So Russia was now at peace. Lenin said that peace would give the Bolsheviks a 'breathing space' which would help them get a grip on the country. But hardly had the Bolsheviks drawn breath when they were faced with a different but just as damaging kind of war – a civil war.

Russian lands lost by the Treaty of Brest-Litovsk, March 1918

Work section

A. Test your understanding of this chapter by explaining the meanings of: decree, Sovnarkom, Cheka, Constituent Assembly, treaty.

B. Study the map above and the terms of the Treaty of Brest-Litovsk, then answer these questions:
1. Which lands did Russia lose by the Treaty?
2. What harmful effects do you think the Treaty had on Russia?
3. Why do you think Lenin agreed to the Treaty of Brest-Litovsk, even though it was so harsh?

C. 1. What advantages of Bolshevik rule can you see in the decrees of Sovnarkom on the opposite page?
2. In your opinion what price did people have to pay for these advantages?

12
CIVIL WAR AND FOREIGN INTERVENTION

No sooner had Lenin and the Bolsheviks made peace with Germany, than enemies of the Bolsheviks inside Russia got ready to fight them. Serious fighting began in May 1918 when anti-Bolshevik soldiers took control of the Trans-Siberian Railway, Russia's vital link between east and west.

The Czech Legion

During May 1918, 45,000 Czech prisoners of war were being taken across Russia on trains to Vladivostok. There they would be put on to ships and sent back to their country by sea. On the way, one trainload of Czechs got into a quarrel with the Soviet of a town on the railway. The quarrel became a fight and the Czechs took control of the town. When Bolshevik troops arrived to restore order, more trainloads of Czech prisoners of war joined in the fight. Within two weeks they had taken over all important towns in the area. By the end of 1918 nearly all the Trans-Siberian Railway and the towns along its route were in Czech hands.

Enemies of the Bolsheviks rushed to join the Czech Legion. Under Czech protection they set up their own governments and claimed that they ruled Russia. The most important of these new governments was called **Komuch**, short for Committee of Members of the Constituent Assembly. Komuch quickly organised the enemies of the Bolsheviks into a People's Army which advanced on Moscow. On the way it captured 650 million gold roubles in an attack on the government's gold reserve at Kazan.

The Bolshevik government, which by now had moved to Moscow, took desperate measures to protect itself. First it introduced conscription. This means that men aged eighteen to forty had to serve in a new Bolshevik army – the **Red Army**. Leon Trotsky was given the job of organising it. Trotsky's first problem was to find officers to lead the Red Army, for most of the troops were raw recruits. His solution was to appoint former officers of the Tsar's army. If they refused, they were sent to prison camps. Any officer who tried deserting to the enemy found his family taken hostage and kept in prison.

Russia during the Civil War, 1918–20

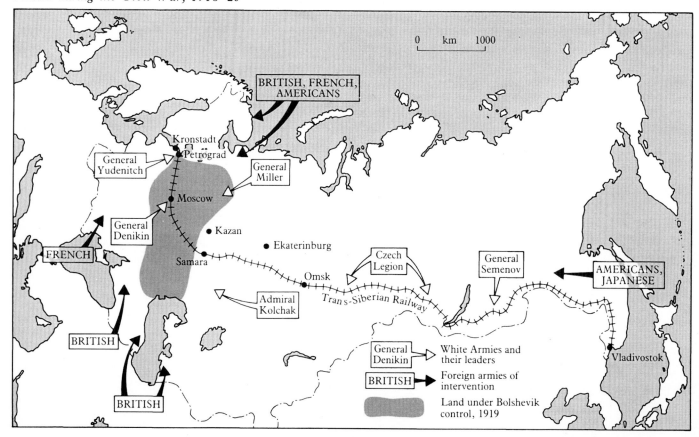

Using these methods Trotsky managed to find 22,000 officers to command the 330,000 men of the Red Army.

Reds and Whites

Against the Red Army, or 'Reds' as they were known, was a great variety of enemies known as '**Whites**'. They were called Whites because white was the traditional colour of the Tsar. In fact, not all Whites were supporters of the Tsar. Many were Socialist Revolutionaries, others were democrats, some were landlords who had been thrown off their land, others were nobles. The White Armies included anyone who opposed the Bolsheviks.

By the end of 1918 four White Armies were attacking the heartland of Russia which was held by the Bolsheviks. They were helped by foreign armies which had been sent by the Allies – the countries on whose side Russia had fought in the Great War. The Allies were angry at Russia's withdrawal from the war and wanted to crush the Bolshevik government. So in addition to the White Armies, the Red Army had to face foreign 'armies of intervention' from Britain, France, America and Japan.

Fighting between the Reds and Whites in the Russian Civil War was often very savage. Many thousands of people on both sides were killed, including civilians. Among the many casualties were the ex-Tsar and his family, who were now prisoners of the Bolsheviks in Ekaterinburg, a town in the Ural mountains (see map opposite). In July 1918 it seemed as if the town would be captured by the Czech Legion. The Bolsheviks feared that the ex-Tsar would be saved and would become the leader of the White Armies. Rather than risk that, the local Bolsheviks shot Nicholas dead, along with his wife Alexandra, their son Alexis, their four daughters and their servants.

The Bolsheviks nearly lost their own leader in August 1918. A Socialist Revolutionary named Fanya Kaplan shot Lenin three times at point blank range while he was getting into a car in Moscow. Although the bullets entered his neck, Lenin survived and recovered within weeks. All that Fanya Kaplan achieved by shooting Lenin was to convince the Bolsheviks that ruthless methods were needed to deal with their White enemies. A week after the shooting, Sovnarkom ordered the Cheka, the secret political police, to begin a 'Red Terror'.

The Red Terror

The Cheka, led by Felix Dzerzhinsky, had its headquarters in Lubyanka Street in Moscow. In the cellars of the Lubyanka, Cheka agents tortured prisoners to extract confessions before executing them. Cheka units in the countryside hanged, beat, shot and burned anyone who helped the Whites or fought for them. Before long the name of the Cheka aroused fear even among loyal Bolsheviks.

In the Red Army Leon Trotsky carried out his own form of terror. In 1918 he issued this order:

'1 Every scoundrel who incites anyone to retreat, to desert, or not to fulfil a military order, will be shot.
2 Every soldier of the Red Army who voluntarily deserts his post, will be shot.
3 Every soldier who throws away his rifle or sells part of his equipment will be shot . . .
6 Those guilty of harbouring deserters are liable to be shot.
7 Houses in which deserters are found are liable to be burned down.'

Trotsky meant what he said. When a Red Army battalion tried running away from a battle shortly after this order was made, Trotsky had one in ten of the soldiers shot by firing squad.

Trotsky was not just a tyrant. He was also a very good military leader. He spent much of the Civil War travelling from one area of the fighting to another. From his war train Trotsky directed the movements of the Red Army, delivered supplies, gave encouragement, and dealt with troublemakers. He made sure that the Red Army was an effective and united fighting force.

Gradually the Red Army began to win the Civil War. In 1919 the foreign armies of intervention were withdrawn from Russia, leaving the White Armies to fight alone. The White Armies never came together as a united force, so Trotsky was always able to fight them one at a time. By the end of 1919 only isolated groups of Whites were still fighting. The Bolshevik government was safe for the time being.

Work section

A. Test your understanding of this chapter by explaining the meanings of: the Czech Legion, Reds, Whites, armies of intervention, the Red Terror.

B. Study the map opposite, then answer these questions:
   1. Which foreign countries sent armies of intervention to fight in the Russian Civil War?
   2. In what ways were the White Armies and the armies of intervention in a strong position in 1919? In what ways were they in a weak position?

C. Study Trotsky's order to the Red Army above. According to this document, what seems to have been the main problem from which the Red Army was suffering in 1918?

13

'ONE STEP BACKWARDS . . .' WAR COMMUNISM AND THE NEP

Starving Russian children photographed in Samara, October 1921

During the Civil War the Bolsheviks took strict measures to organise industry and food supplies in the areas under their control. They had two aims: to keep the Red Army supplied with food and weapons, and to introduce a system of communism – the equal sharing of wealth. These measures were together known as War Communism.

War Communism

There were five aspects of War Communism:

1. All factories with more than ten workers were nationalised – that is, taken over by the government. A government body called Vesenkha (the Supreme Council of National Economy) decided exactly what each industry should produce.
2. All workers were under government control. There was military discipline in the factories, including the death penalty for strikers. The unemployed were made to join 'Labour Armies', cutting trees or building roads, for example.
3. Private trading was banned. Peasants had to give their surplus food to the government: they could not sell it for profit.

4. The government allowed money to lose its value through inflation. It abolished rents, railway fares, postal charges and many other money payments. In place of money, people were encouraged to barter.
5. In cities food was strictly rationed.

War Communism succeeded in one of its aims: the Red Army was kept supplied with food and weapons and, as you have read, it won the Civil War in 1920. But War Communism failed in its other aim – to share Russia's wealth equally. Joseph Stalin, one of the Bolshevik leaders later wrote:

'The best times then were considered to be the days on which we could distribute to the workers of Leningrad and Moscow one-eighth of a pound of black bread, and even that was half bran. And this continued . . . for two whole years.'

What had gone wrong? In the countryside, many peasants decided that there was no point in growing more food than they needed for themselves. Why bother, when War Communism took away their

30

surplus crops? So in 1919 the peasants started to sow less grain and breed fewer animals. The result was a food shortage in 1920 and then a terrible famine in 1921. Starvation, cold weather and disease killed a total of seven million Russians. According to *Pravda*, the Communists' own newspaper, twenty-five million Russians were living below subsistence level.

The New Economic Policy

In March 1921 there was a revolt of 10,000 sailors at **Kronstadt**, a naval base near Petrograd. Kronstadt had been loyal to the Bolsheviks ever since the Revolution, but now the sailors said that War Communism was not what the Bolsheviks had promised in 1917. They got ready to attack Petrograd.

Leon Trotsky and other Red Army generals surrounded Kronstadt with 60,000 troops. They bombed the naval base and then attacked the sailors' headquarters. Many sailors were killed in hand-to-hand fighting. The rest were captured and later shot by the Cheka.

The Kronstadt rising was crushed, but Lenin realised that a change of policy was needed if there were to be no more risings like it. In March 1921 Lenin abandoned War Communism and introduced the **New Economic Policy**, or NEP, in its place. The NEP said that

1. Peasants could sell their surplus food for profit again.
2. Peasants who increased their food production would pay less tax.
3. Factories with fewer than twenty workers would be given back to their owners.
4. People could use money once again.

Many Bolsheviks were shocked by the NEP. They said it was a step backwards towards the old capitalist system. Lenin said that by taking one step backwards they would later be able to take two steps forward towards communism.

By 1925 the NEP had begun to work. As these figures show, food production went back up to the level it had been at before the Great War, while industrial output increased dramatically.

	1913	1922	1925
Grain harvest (millions of tonnes)	80.1	50.3	72.5
Cattle (millions)	58.9	45.8	62.1
Pigs (millions)	20.3	12.0	21.8
Coal (millions of tonnes)	29.0	9.5	18.1
Iron (millions of tonnes)	4.2	0.1	1.5

The 1923 Constitution

At the start of 1923 Russia gained a new constitution and, with it, a new name. The 1923 Constitution said that Russia was a '**Union of Soviet Socialist Republics**'. The country was now a union of four republics – Russia, Byelorussia, the Ukraine and the Caucasus. Each republic had its own government with control over such matters as public health, welfare and education. The national government in Moscow, Sovnarkom, retained control over national concerns such as the armed forces, industry, communications and the secret police.

Lenin's death

Lenin did not live to see the USSR grow to be one of the great powers of the twentieth century world. In 1922 and 1923 he suffered a series of strokes and, in January 1924, he died at the age of fifty-three.

Lenin was not buried or cremated after his funeral. His body was embalmed and put on display in a tomb in Red Square in Moscow. Every year since his death, millions of visitors from all over the USSR and from other countries have queued to see Lenin's body, a sign that he is regarded in the USSR as one of the greatest leaders of the twentieth century.

Work section

A. Test your understanding of this chapter by explaining: War Communism, Kronstadt, the NEP, the USSR.

B. Read the extract on page 30 from Joseph Stalin's *History of the Civil War*.
1. What, according to Stalin, were the 'best times' for city workers during the Civil War?
2. Describe what you think bad times were like for city workers during these years, 1918–20.

C. Study the figures above of agricultural and industrial output.
1. Why did the number of pigs and cattle in Russia drop between 1913 and 1922?
2. Why did the grain harvest fall during these years?
3. What caused the output of industry and agriculture to rise again between 1922 and 1925?

D. Study the photograph opposite. Using your imagination, as well as the information in this chapter, answer these questions:
1. Why do you think these children are so poorly dressed? Where do you think their parents might be?
2. For what purposes do you think this photograph was taken? Explain your answer.

Revision guide

These note headings and sub-headings are designed as a framework for notes which you make for yourself from Chapters 11 to 13. They are not a complete set of notes to be copied.

K. Problems facing the Bolsheviks at the end of 1917

L. The first decrees of Sovnarkom

M. The Constituent Assembly
   1. The elections of 1917
   2. The closing of the Assembly

N. The Treaty of Brest-Litovsk
   1. The peace conference
   2. The terms of the treaty

O. The Civil War and the Intervention
   1. The Czech Legion
   2. Komuch
   3. The creation of the Red Army
   4. The Whites
   5. The armies of intervention
   6. The execution of the royal family
   7. The Red Terror
   8. The victory of the Bolsheviks

P. War Communism
   1. The policies
   2. The famine of 1921

Q. The Kronstadt rising, 1921

R. The New Economic Policy
   1. The policy
   2. The results

S. The 1923 constitution

T. Lenin's death

Revision exercise

Study this comparison of Russia before 1917 with Russia after 1917, then answer the questions beneath.

	Before 1917	After 1917
Government and Politics		
The country	The Russian Empire	The Union of Soviet Socialist Republics (from 1923)
The form of government	An autocracy	A dictatorship
The leader	Tsar Nicholas II	Sovnarkom (Chairman = Lenin)
Parliament	The Duma	The Congress of Soviets
Voting	Property owners could vote	All adults could vote
Political parties	Some parties allowed, but no revolutionary parties	Only the Bolshevik Party (called Communist Party after 1918) allowed
Society		
The peasants	Did not own land	Owned land
Industrial workers	On average, worked eleven hours a day, sixty-six hours a week.	On average, worked eight hours a day, forty-eight hours a week
Nobles	Owned a great deal of land; had power and influence	Land confiscated; no political power
Capitalists	Owned factories, mines, banks etc.	Banks, factories, etc. confiscated
Rights and freedoms		
The press	Press censored	Press censored and under government control
Religion	Freedom of belief; church under state control	Russia a non-religious state; no links between church and state
Foreign relations	Russia had many allies. Involved in two wars: with Japan 1904–5; and the Great War, 1914–17	No allies. Involved in Civil War 1918–20 and in the 'wars of intervention', 1918–19

1. What similarities are there between Russia before 1917 and Russia after 1917?
2. In what ways did Russia change after the Bolshevik revolution of 1917?
3. In your opinion, did Russians benefit from Bolshevik rule after 1917? Explain your answer.